• Compiled by his wife: Margo Schoder •

RIGHTLY DISCERNING THE COVENANTS

IN LOVING MEMORY

WARREN REX SCHODER

RIGHTLY DISCERNING THE COVENANTS
In loving memory of the author / Warren Schoder
Compiled by his wife / Margo Schoder
Copyright © 2024 Margo Schoder
ISBN: 978-1-964359-04-5
LCCN: 2024917961

All rights reserved. No part of this book may be reproduced, stored in a retrieval system, or transmitted in any form or by any means—electronic, mechanical, digital, photocopy, or any other—without prior permission from the publisher and author, except as provided by the United States of America copyright law.

Unless otherwise noted, all scriptures are from the KING JAMES VERSION, public domain.

Scripture quotations marked (NAS) are taken from the NEW AMERICAN STANDARD BIBLE®, Copyright© 1960, 1962, 1963, 1968, 1971, 1972, 1973, 1975, 1977, 1995 by The Lockman Foundation. Used by permission.

Individuals and church groups may order books from Margo Schoder directly, or from the publisher. Retailers and wholesalers should order from our distributors. Refer to the Deeper Revelation Books website for distribution information, as well as an online catalog of all our books.

Author Warren Schoder graduated to heaven November 5th, 2023. His wife of 55 years, Margo Schoder, discovered this manuscript after his demise and determined to publish it and assist in establishing his legacy. Her email address is: dhglory3@gmail.com.

Published by:
Deeper Revelation Books
Revealing "the deep things of God" (1 Cor. 2:10)
P.O. Box 4260
Cleveland, TN 37320 423-478-2843
Website: www.deeperrevelationbooks.org
Email: info@deeperrevelationbooks.org

Deeper Revelation Books and its divisions assist Christian writers in publishing and distributing their works. Our authors are the ultimate decision-makers in the process. Final responsibility for the creative design, content, permissions, editorial accuracy, stories and doctrinal views, either expressed or implied, belongs to the author. What you hold in your hand is an expression of this author's passion to publish the truth to this generation with a spirit of excellence. It was a blessing and an honor to assist in this process.

FOREWORD

I have known Warren Schoder for more than forty years as a trusted friend, coworker in our ministry, gifted Bible teacher, devoted husband and father. As God would have it, Warren graduated to heaven on my birthday in 2023, after which I was thrilled to learn his beloved wife, Margo, had discovered that Warren had left a manuscript that is now the book you are reading.

As a Christian church that strongly supports Israel, celebrates the New Covenant aspects of Passover and the Feast of Tabernacles, we have been closely associated with Messianic churches and prominent Jewish leaders, making the subject of this book relevant to our close friendships and the unity we strive to cultivate.

In Warren's study of the Old and New Covenants, he gives us a thoughtful and balanced view of the messages of law and grace and cautions us against adopting a performance-based Gospel. His careful application of Scripture helps us understand the freedom we have been given through Jesus' sacrifice on the cross ... not diminishing the purpose of the Old Testament to make us aware of our need for a Savior, but showing us that Jesus fulfilled the law, removing its burden from the believer.

This vital study serves to promote unity between both Jewish and Gentile believers, steering us away from deception and gently guiding us back to the joy of our salvation. May you gain insight and encouragement from its pages.

Phil Derstine
Senior Pastor
The Family Church at Christian Retreat
Bradenton, Florida

Pastor Phil Derstine and Warren

DEDICATION

First of all, I dedicate this book to my Lord and Savior, in honor of my beloved husband. Second I dedicate this book to our family, friends and my church family who have always been there for us.

To our amazing nieces and nephews loved by their Uncle Warren and I who brought so much joy and love into our lives over many years. Thank you for being such a precious part of our family and who made Uncle Warren's life so special and mine too. You even named his boat the SS UNCLE WARREN.

To our daughter Susan and son David, thank you so much for sacrificing your lives to be with your Dad and I during these most difficult times. I appreciate you both more than you could ever imagine. I love you both so much.

Love, **Mom**

Daughter Susan and son David

ACKNOWLEDGEMENT

Joanne Derstine Curphey, I am so thankful to have a friend like you who would help me honor Warren's legacy by helping to edit his book. Your contribution is a beautiful tribute to his memory.

LEGACY

To my Sweet love, God's got this!

Warren left a legacy that will continue to influence the lives of others. I want to take the time to honor my husband who has gone to be with JESUS by sharing something close to my heart. My honey was the rock and foundation, not only to our family, but also to our extended family. Being married fifty-five years is rare these days.

I believe we were able to minister to younger couples by our loving commitment to each other as a married couple. We surely had our ups and downs throughout life, but, with God's grace, we experienced His amazing forgiveness. Over decades of our married life, we were always reassured of God's promise that He would never leave us or forsake us. By God's grace, our marriage endured, and we served as living examples of God's persevering grace to the coming generations of married couples. He always called me his "SWEET LOVE."

I will forever love you.

Margo

TABLE OF CONTENTS

PREFACE 11
INTRODUCTION 13
THE GOSPEL OF JESUS CHRIST
A Simple Message 17
MAINTAINING A
GOOD FOUNDATION 21
AN EVIL AGENDA
The Little Foxes Spoil the Vine 27
WORD REDEFINITION
A Fundamental Tool of Deception 31
THE MEANING AND PURPOSE
OF A COVENANT 35
PARTIES TO A COVENANT
Who Is Speaking and to
Whom Is It Being Spoken? 37
THE SAVED OR THE UNSAVED? 41
THE OLD TESTAMENT
A Covenant of Works
Through the Flesh 45
THE NEW TESTAMENT
Grace Through Faith 49
THE OLD COVENANT
A Finished Work 53
FULFILLED: What Does It Mean? 55
HALLELUJAH! 59

FRUSTRATING THE GRACE OF GOD 61

THE LAW VERSUS FAITH
It's One or the Other 65

OUR RESPONSE (RELATIONSHIP)
TO THE OLD COVENANT 61

CAN IT GET ANY CLEARER
THAN THIS? 73

HIGHER GROUND 79

SUMMING IT ALL UP 83

LOVING MEMORIES 89

A SONG WARREN WROTE 91

EULOGY: MY DAD
by Warren's son, David Schoder 93

A LOVING NOTE
by Warren's grandson, Noah Schoder 99

BIOGRAPHICAL SUMMARY 101

PHOTO ALBUM 105

PREFACE

As we approach the end of the age, the plan of God to bring together the Jew (circumcision) and non-Jew (uncircumcision) is becoming better recognized, accepted, and embraced by the church. Christian believers are developing a genuine interest in understanding the origins of their faith and, in a desire to be one with Jewish believers, are extending to them the true love of Jesus Christ. The author shares this love for the Jew and for Israel.

A reciprocal part of this outreach is that Christians are receiving a greater understanding about the origins of their faith from their Jewish brethren. More and more, leaders of Messianic congregations are "crossing over" with Christian church leaders to share their respective insights one group to the other.

The purpose of this writing is to help Jewish and non-Jewish believers alike recognize that much of the "unity" coming about through these interactions is, in fact, inconsistent with and even contrary to the plan of God to bring about "one new man," as described by the Apostle Paul in Ephesians 2:15.

A vital key to God's marvelous redemption plan lies in rightly discerning the covenants. The Old and New Testaments were each given for a very specific purpose. Failure to recognize this important purpose will leave us vulnerable to deception and allow us to be led seriously astray.

The people of God must never lose sight of Satan's commitment to undermining the plan of God. He is crafty and wiley, but "we are not ignorant of his devices." (2 Corinthians 2:11) In the pages that follow, I hope to show the way in which the "one new man" teaching throughout much of the body of Christ has been misunderstood and incorrectly taught. By rightly discerning the covenants, we can be sure that the blood which Jesus so willingly shed for us will not have been in vain.

INTRODUCTION

One of the most perplexing Bible questions in the minds of Christian believers pertains to the Old Testament or the "law" and its applicability to our lives today. Time and time again, we hear instruction about our need to fulfill the law in our lives and how, through the power of the Holy Spirit, we are now to strive to comply with its mandates.

Relatively few of these teachings speak of obedience to the law as a salvation requirement but a good many tell us that, once we are saved, we have the ability to obey the law and should do so. Since the Old Covenant dealt with the Jewish people, and since Jesus Christ ministered under the Old Covenant and fulfilled it flawlessly, many current day teachings emphasize the need for us to return to our "Hebraic roots." This is to be done by digging back into the law or "torah," as many are calling it, so that we can walk out our righteousness.

Frequently, this particular emphasis arises from an involvement with Messianic congregations which typically follow many of the Old Covenant traditions to varying degrees. Often, in a desire to show oneness with Jewish believers, converted Gentiles will join with these seekers at their weekly Shabbat (Sabbath) services either on a Friday evening or Saturday. Conversely,

Messianic teachers – often addressed as Rabbi – are invited to share with their non-Jewish brothers and, in so doing, introduce and share many of their Old Testament insights.

Arising from this crossover is a sect of non-Jewish believers that are now teaching about the importance of "torah" and raising up "torah observant" congregations. In their zeal to embrace and teach a new revelation, Christian seekers actively pursue this pathway without realizing their departure from Gospel fundamentals. Simple New Testament truth is either ignored or rationalized away in order to sustain this deceptive "other gospel."

Tragically, the torah movement is being propagated through sincere people who "have a zeal of God, but not according to knowledge." (Romans 10:2) The tragedy is that they desperately seek to find life in a place where it can never be found:

> *"For if there had been a law given which could have given life, verily righteousness should have been by the law."*
> (Galatians 3:21)

As a consequence, those who pursue this often see the joy of their salvation slipping away but don't know where it went. Even though they want more of Jesus, sadly, they are looking for it in His shadow instead of in His presence.

Unfortunately, many young converts without a sufficient grasp of salvation basics are being drawn off into this dead, lifeless theology.

This message is written, not because the body needs more information to read, but from a passion stirred by the Holy Spirit to bring a clear, Biblical teaching on a subject that has long been ignored or incorrectly taught. As you read, you will notice that this writing is not founded on personal opinion but, rather, on a compilation of Biblical teachings that, hopefully, will put to rest any confusion you previously had about a subject that the Bible presents in a simple, easy-to-understand manner. Please read prayerfully – asking that the Holy Spirit would remove any scales and impart revelation.

THE GOSPEL OF JESUS CHRIST: A Simple Message

The developments discussed above should not really come to us as a surprise. In these perilous last days, we know that:

"Seducers shall wax worse and worse, deceiving, and being deceived."
(2 Timothy 3:13)

But, perhaps the most difficult reality to accept is that the deception will frequently come to us through those to whom we are the closest and who we esteem highly as teachers and leaders.

When our spiritual life seems to be getting cluttered and complicated, the first step should be to quickly retreat to the Word and prayer and find out where we have gone astray. Paul, in dealing with the deceptions that were coming into the Corinthian church, expressed it well when he wrote:

"But I fear, lest by any means, as the serpent beguiled Eve through his subtilty, so your minds should be corrupted from the simplicity that is in Christ. For if he that cometh preacheth another Jesus, whom we have not preached, or if ye receive another spirit, which ye have not received,

or another gospel, which ye have not accepted, ye might well bear with him."
(2 Corinthians 11:3-4)

A simple message has no appeal to the natural man because it does not contain the intellectual component that satisfies the pride of the flesh. Paul understood this and recognized that, through subtle deviations, the Corinthian believers could be easily led astray. Knowing the vulnerability of his flesh, he guarded himself as indicated in 1 Corinthians 2:1-5 when he wrote:

"And I, brethren, when I came to you, came not with excellency of speech or of wisdom, declaring unto you the testimony of God. For I determined not to know any thing among you, save Jesus Christ, and him crucified. And I was with you in weakness, and in fear, and in much trembling. And my speech and my preaching was not with enticing words of man's wisdom, but in demonstration of the Spirit and of power: That your faith should not stand in the wisdom of men, but in the power of God."

Note that "**enticing words**" are not given to us by God. Enticing words are words with a particular agenda that spring forth from "**man's wisdom**," and which are contrary to the plan and purpose of God.

The Bible is well able to speak for itself. In almost every case where diverse doctrines are being taught, it is because someone has deviated from the straight and narrow path of truth to satisfy some pet teaching. Once this happens, the Bible must now be twisted and manipulated to conform to this new "revelation."

Point #1

Ask yourself if the simplicity of the Gospel message is still there. Does the Word preached still contain the sound, crisp power of Christ's shed blood, death, and resurrection, or has this vital, fundamental truth been relegated to the back seat and displaced by an alternate doctrine? If that pure, essential simplicity is missing, then your faith is being built on man's wisdom and not God's. Is the focal point of the message in agreement with the New Testament emphasis on grace and faith?

Point #2

Is the Bible being used to support the message in a responsible, non-manipulative way? One telltale sign of variance is when words are being played with, definitions stretched, and fancy catchphrases used to support the deviant doctrine. This tells us that the teaching cannot stand on its own but needs to be propped up.

MAINTAINING A GOOD FOUNDATION

Essential for the strength of our spiritual house is the maintaining of a good foundation. A foundation that is not maintained will deteriorate and, over time, allow the whole superstructure to topple. Any deterioration begins with just a small crack. A foundation wall needs only to admit the smallest amount of moisture. Frost then hardens the moisture causing the outer, protective foundation coating to crack wider and admit more moisture – and so on.

In our walk with Jesus, maintaining a good foundation means rightly dividing the Word of Truth and holding fast to the essential truths that brought us to Christ in the first place. A backslidden Christian is one who has allowed the smallest amount of untruth to creep in and to begin eroding that vital foundation. The acceptance of one untruth opens the door for another to enter. In a short period of time, the entire spiritual foundation has been compromised and we can literally find ourselves entangled in heresy. This is why we are admonished in Hebrews 10:23 to:

"Hold fast the profession of our faith without wavering; (for he is faithful that promised;)."

What profession? Our profession of **faith**.

Proper use and interpretation of Scripture is of foremost importance if we are to avoid pitfalls in our understanding. A fundamental element is recognizing the fact that revelation is progressive. That is, there is a greater degree of revelation in the New Testament than what we find in the old.

> *"For this cause I Paul, the prisoner of Jesus Christ for you Gentiles, If ye have heard of the dispensation of the grace of God which is given me to you-ward: How that by revelation he made known unto me the mystery; (as I wrote afore in few words, Whereby, when ye read, ye may understand my knowledge in the mystery of Christ) Which in other ages was not made known unto the sons of men, as it is now revealed unto his holy apostles and prophets by the Spirit."* (Ephesians 3:1-5)

> *"God, who at sundry times and in divers manners spake in time past unto the fathers by the prophets, Hath in these last days spoken unto us by his Son, whom he hath appointed heir of all things, by whom also he made the worlds."* (Hebrews 1:1-2)

The above scriptures should alert us to the fallacy of trying to use the Old Testament to illuminate the new. The problem here is that a shadow has no light of its own. The Old Testament is not the real. It was given to **point the way** to the real. But it is only a shadow, a pattern, a figure, and an example of the real. (Hebrews 8:5; Hebrews 10:1;

Colossians 2:17) To get a clearer understanding of that which cast the shadow, we don't examine the shadow more closely. Instead, we look at that which cast the shadow since only it has the detail and definition that enables us to fully comprehend that which the shadow represents.

> *"Now of the things which we have spoken this is the sum: We have such an high priest, who is set on the right hand of the throne of the Majesty in the heavens; A minister of the sanctuary, and of the **true tabernacle**, which the Lord pitched, and not man."* (Hebrews 8:1-2)

> *"For Christ is not entered into the holy places made with hands, which are the **figures of the true**; but into heaven itself, now to appear in the presence of God for us."* (Hebrews 9:24)

> *"For if he were on earth, he should not be a priest, seeing that there are priests that offer gifts according to the law: Who serve unto the **example and shadow of heavenly things**, as Moses was admonished of God when he was about to make the tabernacle: for, See, saith he, that thou make all things according to the **pattern** shewed to thee in the mount."* (Hebrews 8:4-5)

The people of God in times past had a degree of understanding about spiritual truth. But when Jesus came to earth and left us His Holy Spirit after His resurrection, a new level of revelation concerning spiritual mysteries was given. This being the case, we must give greater place to New Testament truth, recognizing that it is the new and true to which the Old Testament was pointing.

The reason we are admonished to hold fast the profession of our faith without wavering (Hebrews 10:23) is because the enemy's mission is:

> *"To steal, and to kill, and to destroy."* (John 10:10)

If he can, he will direct us down a side road to keep us from fulfilling the plan and purpose of God for our lives.

The speed at which we can be overcome by doctrinal deception is most alarming. Paul acknowledged his concern about this when he wrote to the believers at the Galatian church:

> *"I marvel that ye are so soon removed from him that called you into the grace of Christ unto **another gospel**."* (Galatians 1:6)

The concern expressed here is clearly – **abandoning grace**. This was not happening on its own but, rather, as a result of concerted efforts by those with an evil agenda who came in secretly to spy on the believers and divert them from Gospel truth so as to bring them back under the bondage of the law.

> *"And that because of false brethren unawares brought in, who came in privily to spy out our liberty which we have in Christ Jesus, that they might bring us into bondage."* (Galatians 2:4)

The grace message is an offense to the one who is steeped in performance since the way we appropriate grace is through faith and not works. If there are no works, then there is no place for boasting or pride. (Ephesians 2:8-9) To satisfy the flesh, the law must remain in place with all its associated dos and don'ts. This way, one can compare himself with others and be puffed up in those areas where he excels.

*"For the law having a **shadow** of good things to come, and **not the very image of the things**, can never with those sacrifices which they offered year by year continually make the comers thereunto perfect."* (Hebrews 10:1)

*"Let no man therefore judge you in meat, or in drink, or in respect of an holyday, or of the new moon, or of the sabbath days: Which are **a shadow of things to come**; but the body is of Christ."* (Colossians 2:16-17)

AN EVIL AGENDA:
The Little Foxes Spoil the Vine

As was seen earlier, a deviation from the true Gospel message always springs forth from an evil agenda. This may not be a conscious effort on the part of the one bringing the false message; but it is always a deliberate, conscious agenda on the part of the enemy of our souls who has perpetrated the deceptive message.

The recent torah teachings referenced earlier are riddled with subtleties designed to initially separate the believer from key, Gospel truths. Most blatant and obvious is the replacing of the word "**law**" with the Hebrew word "***torah***" – giving it a new and expanded meaning.

These messages encourage Christian believers to connect with Hebraic roots through a renewed focus on torah. Torah, we are told, doesn't just mean "the law," but by broadened definition is "the teaching and instruction of God." As such, it encompasses not just the five books of the law or even all the Scripture writings penned before Christ. Now, through this new definition, many teach that torah includes even the four gospels and the epistles.

At face value, the use of torah as a substitute for law would appear innocuous and a relatively minor matter. After all, *torah* is the Hebrew word that is translated law. **The subsequent melding of the new and old covenants that emerges from this redefinition, however, is another issue entirely and is clearly the agenda behind the word substitution**. It is here where the message departs directly and rapidly from Biblical truth and, in fact, becomes "**another gospel**." (Galatians 1:6)

This stark contradiction is found in the fact that the epistles, in particular, make **clear**, **specific**, and **emphatic** distinctions between the old and new covenants, i.e., their purpose, attributes, provisions, etc. By running these together under the heading "the teaching and instruction of God," the uniqueness of each covenant is blurred, and the hearer is left believing that there is no difference. They have now simply become "the Word of God." To compile torah doctrine on top of such a false underlying premise is to distort and deceive. Half-truths hardly constitute responsible Bible teaching.

Further reinforcement of this comes when torah teachers are left with no choice but to simply ignore these New Testament teachings or try to bring them into agreement with the first error through either weak rationalizations or further interpretive distortions. **The only problem with this manner of instruction is that it leaves out very important distinctions, made within the Bible itself, which provide further qualification and clarification about "the Word of God."** This amounts to "subtracting from" what is written – a gross mishandling of God's Word which can hardly be characterized as "rightly dividing the word of truth."

WORD REDEFINITION:
A Fundamental Tool of Deception

Word redefinition, it should be noted, is a long-standing New World Order tactic employed by governments, media, and NGO agencies to mold public opinion and to implement specific agendas. Political figures with global leadership aspirations, in particular, are keenly aware of the power of words in helping to draw public opinion towards their cause. Consequently, they utilize word change tactics frequently and craftily to sway opinion – often away from truth – towards a specific agenda.

One glaring example of this is the change which came about in the early part of the 20th century wherein media and political leaders began referring to the United States as a "democracy" instead of a "republic." Unknown to many, the founders of our great nation gave us a republic, not a democracy. The problem this presents for today's free-thinking political establishment is that a republic is guided and constrained by the provisions of the constitution that governs it. For those seeking to operate outside those constraints, public attention must first be diverted away from their intentions. This takes place primarily through the media and educational systems by reshaping public perception and awareness through the subtle introduction of what, today, is called "politically correct" language.

While the word "democracy" has pleasant connotations – inferring fairness and equality, in reality, a democracy is nothing more than mob rule. It speaks to the idea that the will of the majority is more important than the legal provisions of the constitution. Probably few ever recognized the word substitution when it was introduced but this subtle alteration eroded, in the minds of the American people, the significance of the Constitution in maintaining a strong, ethical standard for both present and future generations. As such, it paved the way for the courts of the land to give greater credence to mass consensus than to the laws on which our nation was founded.

Sad to say, modern Hebrew interpretation has progressed to the point where, through sufficient "research," words can ultimately come to mean anything you want them to. Surely this is a dangerous practice and one against which a child of God should be alert and discerning.

Catchy clichés like "torah-based" and "torah-observant" appear nowhere in Scripture. Rather, they are words that torah teachers often use to try to bridge the obstacle of rigid compliance presented by the law. But the law makes no provision for such partial attempts to fulfill it. So long as the law is in place, it must be obeyed to a "T" or we become subject to its penalties.

"And the law is not of faith: but, the

man that doeth them shall live in them."
(Galatians 3:12)

Once place is given to word manipulation, the door swings open to outright fabrication. One example of this is seen when Jesus is referred to as the "living torah." Not only does this term not appear in the Bible, it is actually a contradiction since the Bible tells us that **the law cannot bring life**.

"For if there had been a law given which could have given life, verily righteousness should have been by the law."
(Galatians 3:21)

THE MEANING AND PURPOSE OF A COVENANT

A key to understanding the above fallacy lies in recognizing that God's Word is given to us in "**covenants**." A covenant is clearly the word of the person or persons signing or ratifying it. But covenants include terms and conditions that clarify the intent and application of the words contained therein. These provisions include such things as: who the covenant pertains to, start date, end date, penalties for failure to fulfill, etc. **To take words spoken in a covenant and disassociate them with the stated terms, conditions, and fulfillment criteria is to distort their meaning and send a message inconsistent with the words of the covenant**.

We could say, for instance, that a mortgage covenant is your agreement with the mortgage lender about the responsibilities each party has to the other pertaining to the loan being granted. As the "mortgagor" (debtor) making payments to the "mortgagee" (lender), you are obligated to continue those payments for a specific period of time and until the full balance is paid off if you wish to continue living in your home. Once all the conditions are met, however, the agreement is "fulfilled." From this point on, the home is yours, and you are under no further obligation to continue making payments.

PARTIES TO THE COVENANT: Who Is Speaking and to Whom Is It Being Spoken?

"**I'm not talking to you**" is a phrase we might hear when a bystander to a conversation responds to a comment not spoken to him. A mistake commonly and easily made when interpreting Scripture is to fail to identify who is speaking, who is being spoken to, and under what covenant someone is operating when the words are being spoken. The fact that your neighbor's car loan contract requires $450.00 per month be paid to the finance company doesn't cause you to sit down and write a $450.00 check to the finance company. Why? Because your name isn't on the contract. In other words, that document isn't talking to you. You have no obligation to it and are in no danger of threats from the finance company for nonpayment.

But, when it comes to interpreting Scripture, believers are all too ready to follow instructions not being given to them. Such failure to recognize the defined parties to God's covenants is a dangerous pitfall when it comes to rightly dividing the Word of Truth and brings about much unnecessary confusion among believers.

A good example of this is in Romans 3:19. In the first two chapters of Romans and the early part of chapter 3, Paul discusses the matters of the law, the benefits for those that follow it, and the penalties for those who don't. His ultimate conclusion, however, is that:

"There is none righteous, no, not one." (Romans 3:10)

But, in verse 19, we see that the law was never given as a means by which people would come into relationship with God but, rather, as a means by which the guilt of all mankind would be firmly and irrefutably established. Only when confronted with his wretched, depraved, and hopeless condition can man comprehend his need for a Savior. Once that revelation has been received, however, the truth of God's grace made known, and Jesus is received by faith, the work of the law in our lives is complete. Hence, Paul goes on to say:

"Now we know that what things soever the law saith, it saith to them who are under the law: that every mouth may be stopped, and all the world may become guilty before God." (Romans 3:19)

To make sure there's no misunderstanding about where we stand in all of this, Paul gives clarification:

"For sin shall not have dominion over you: for ye are not under the law, but under grace." (Romans 6:14)

When a sinner gives his life to Jesus and becomes "**born again**," he receives righteousness as a free gift from God. (Romans 5:15-18) He is now the righteousness of God in Christ and according to what Paul wrote to Timothy, the law is not made for a righteous man.

"Knowing this, that the law is not made for a righteous man, but for the lawless and disobedient, for the ungodly and for sinners, for unholy and profane, for murderers of fathers and murderers of mothers, for manslayers." (1 Timothy 1:9)

THE SAVED OR THE UNSAVED?

Confusion regarding the law and grace also arises from a misunderstanding about what the Bible teaches concerning "righteousness" and how it pertains to the saved and unsaved.

Failure to properly discern and apply this vital truth can quickly divert us from the straight and narrow Gospel path. Paul's teachings, in particular, reveal to us the fact that there are **two** kinds of righteousness. To confuse these and/or not recognize the difference between them is to miss the greatness of what Jesus did on the cross and to remain in needless bondage as a born again child of God.

The two kinds of righteousness spoken of in the Bible are presented most simply and clearly in Philippians 3:9:

> "And be found in him, not having **mine own righteousness**, which is of the law, but that which is through the faith of Christ, **the righteousness which is of God by faith**."

This verse tells us of righteousness:

- **which is of the law** (my own righteousness which I earn through my works)

- **which is by faith** (God's righteousness bestowed on us as a gift from God)

The righteousness which is **of the law** is explained in the Old Testament. The righteousness which is **of God** (**by faith**) is revealed in the New Testament.

> *"For I am not ashamed of the gospel of Christ: for it is the power of God unto salvation to every one that believeth; to the Jew first, and also to the Greek. For **therein** is the righteousness **of God** revealed from faith to faith: as it is written, The just shall live by faith."* (Romans 1:16-17)

The word **therein** above is referring to **the Gospel of Christ** of which Paul says he is not ashamed. Why is it that the natural man is ashamed of and offended by the Gospel of Christ and constantly gravitates back to things of the law? It is because, in acknowledging Jesus, we must admit our own inability, weakness, unworthiness, sinfulness, and unrighteousness. We are lost, wretched, hopeless, and in need of help. We recognize the need for a righteousness that cannot be produced by the works of the flesh. We need **the righteousness of God**.

The righteousness of God, as we just read, is revealed in **the Gospel of Christ** – not in the law. Therefore, if we desire to understand **His** righteousness, we must look to the Gospel or **Good News**. The Good News is that our eternity is no longer dependent on our own righteousness. Because God has given us his righteousness by grace through faith, we are assured of victory and life everlasting. The temptation and seduction continually faced by the believer is to come back under the law; to revert back to works where, once again, pride can rise up and works can try to prove our own worthiness. For this reason, it should not surprise us that many will come teaching that we must fulfill the law once we are saved. This is why Paul admonished the **believers** at the church in Galatia saying:

> *"This only would I learn of you, Received ye the Spirit by the works of the law, or by the hearing of faith? Are ye so foolish? having begun in the Spirit, are ye now made perfect by the flesh?"*
> (Galatians 3:2-3)

Our salvation is not perfected or completed by returning to the law but by continuing the walk of faith in Jesus Christ through the power of the Holy Ghost.

THE OLD TESTAMENT:
A Covenant of Works
Through the Flesh

FLESH and WORKS are the operative words of the Old Testament. Yes – there is provision for forgiveness of sin under the old covenant, but works performance is its underpinning. The Bible clearly makes this point. One primary verse is found in Romans 3:27 which tells us that the law is a law of works:

"Where is boasting then? It is excluded. By what law? of works? Nay: but by the law of faith."

... and that its interaction is with the flesh:

*"For if the blood of bulls and of goats, and the ashes of an heifer sprinkling the unclean, sanctifieth to the **purifying of the flesh**: How much more shall the blood of Christ, who through the eternal Spirit offered himself without spot to God, purge your conscience from dead works to serve the living God?"* (Hebrews 9:13-14)

In John 1:17, we see that grace did not come to us through Moses but through Jesus:

"For the law was given by Moses, but grace and truth came by Jesus Christ."

The old covenant or law of works was not God's **actual** redemption plan. It was an **example** of the redemption that was to come which would actually "purge your conscience from dead works." It demonstrated God's mercy in that those who failed to meet the law's demands could find forgiveness through the atonement of an animal sacrifice. But, as we saw in Hebrews 9:13-14, the old covenant could only sanctify "**to the purifying of the flesh**." The old covenant provided a covering for sins, but through the new covenant, sins are **remitted**, i.e. they are washed away.

The Old Testament was given with a very specific intent and purpose. This intent was not made clear within the Old Testament itself but is well revealed to us in the new. Here we read that **the Old Testament's real purpose** was:

- to stop every mouth that "**all the world may become guilty before God**." (Romans 3:19)
- to "**conclude all under sin**." (Galatians 3:22)
- "**to bring us unto Christ, that we might be justified by faith**." (Galatians 3:24)

But the law had flaws and shortcomings that made it impossible for God's ultimate salvation plan to be manifest through it:

> "For what the law could not do, in that it was weak through the flesh, God sending his own Son in the likeness of sinful flesh, and for sin, condemned sin in the flesh." (Romans 8:3)

Consequently, another or successor plan was needed that would bring about this great salvation plan.

> *"For if the inheritance be of the law, it is no more of promise: but God gave it to Abraham by promise."* (Galatians 3:18)

This was not a new plan that God thought of subsequent to the law. It was, in fact, part of God's original design. But since grace had not yet come, the law was **added** *"till the seed should come to whom the promise was made."* (Galatians 3:19)

> *"And this I say, that the covenant, that was confirmed before of God in Christ, the law, which was four hundred and thirty years after, cannot disannul, that it should make the promise of none effect. For if the inheritance be of the law, it is no more of promise: but God gave it to Abraham by promise. Wherefore then serveth the law? It was **added** because of transgressions, till the seed should come to whom the promise was made; and it was ordained by angels in the hand of a mediator."* (Galatians 3:17-19)

THE NEW TESTAMENT:
Grace Through Faith

GRACE and FAITH are the operative words of the New Testament just as works and the flesh are the operative words of the Old Testament.

> *"For by **grace** are ye saved through **faith**; and that not of yourselves: it is the gift of God: Not of works, lest any man should boast."* (Ephesians 2:8-9)

> *"But God commendeth his love toward us, in that, while we were yet sinners, Christ died for us."* (Romans 5:8)

Contrary to what is often taught, faith is not given to us so we can use it to obey the law. Paul explains this when he says:

> *"And the law is not of faith: but, The man that doeth them shall live in them."* (Galatians 3:12)

The law and faith are two different things just as the Old and New Testaments are two distinct covenants. Performing the works of the law leaves room for pride and boasting. Grace, on the other hand, dispels boasting as there is no work or performance involved in receiving a gift.

The New Testament is the covenant of grace and promise. Faith is the means by which we access God's grace and receive these promises. It is the door through which we must walk to avail ourselves of those things which are freely given to us. The Holy Spirit is the one who brings this revelation.

"Now we have received, not the spirit of the world, but the spirit which is of God; that we might know the things that are freely given to us of God."
(1 Corinthians 2:12)

To hear some speak, we might think that faith just takes us so far and then it's time for works to kick back in. Misinterpretations of James' epistle, in particular, are largely responsible for this error.

Hebrews 11:1 tells us **what** faith is:

"Now faith is the substance of things hoped for, the evidence of things not seen."

But we see **how** faith works in Romans 4:21. Here, where Paul is speaking of Abraham's response to the promise from God that he would be the father of many nations, he says:

*"And being not weak in faith, he considered not his own body now dead, when he was about an hundred years old, neither yet the deadness of Sarah's womb: He staggered not at the promise of God through unbelief; but was strong in faith, giving glory to God; And **being fully persuaded that, what he had promised, he was able also to perform**."* (Romans 4:19-21)

Here we see an excellent definition of what faith actually is. Verse 21 clearly tells us that faith is "being fully persuaded that, what he (God) had promised, he was able also to perform." To be fully persuaded means to know, to be confident of, and to have no doubt about. To have faith in Jesus Christ is to be totally secure in our salvation; to know what Jesus said is true and that God did what He said He would do through Jesus' death on the cross and resurrection.

THE OLD COVENANT:
A Finished Work

One of the most confusing matters for Christian believers is the relationship of the law to our lives today. This is due mostly to the fact that the subject is not being addressed by church leaders and, when it is, it is often not being properly taught. There are a number of reasons for this:

1. Deception

2. Religious spirit

3. Flesh wants to boast

4. Intimidation of the enemy

5. Lack of an intimate relationship with Jesus

Before Jesus gave up the ghost on Calvary's cross, he uttered the words:

"It is finished." (John 19:30)

Embodied in that very statement is the reality that all the terms and provisions of the old covenant had been fulfilled. The work was complete.

*"He **taketh away** the first, that he may establish the second."* (Hebrews 10:9)

This statement tells us that, as long as the first (old) covenant was in force, the second (new) could not be established. The first had to be completed before the second could be started.

Trying to live under the second while still "flirting" with the first, we are told, constitutes nothing less than spiritual bigamy. In Romans chapter 7, the Apostle Paul uses this very analogy about trying to serve the law once we have become believers.

> *"For the woman which hath an husband is bound by the law to her husband so long as he liveth; but if the husband be dead, she is loosed from the law of her husband. So then if, while her husband liveth, she be married to another man, she shall be called an adulteress: but if her husband be dead, she is free from that law; so that she is no adulteress, though she be married to another man."* (Romans 7:2-3)

To make sure we don't miss the correlation here, Paul says:

> *"Wherefore, my brethren, ye also are become dead to the law by the body of Christ; that ye should be married to another, even to him who is raised from the dead, that we should bring forth fruit unto God. For when we were in the flesh, the motions of sins, which were by the law, did work in our members to bring forth fruit unto death. But now we are delivered from the law, that being dead wherein we were held; that we should serve in newness of spirit, and not in the oldness of the letter."* (Romans 7:4-6)

FULFILLED:
What Does It Mean?

"Fulfilled" is another very straightforward word for which religious spirits feel compelled to find an alternate meaning. In natural terms, we have no problem understanding the term "fulfilled." It means to be satisfied, to have all the terms and conditions met, to bring to completion.

Some might expound on this – saying that **fulfill** means "to teach more clearly." In the absence of many other clarifying scriptures, this might be an acceptable interpretation. But the Bible deals with the real meaning so sufficiently that to arrive at a conclusion other than that Jesus "put away" the law is outright rebellion against God's Word. The following scriptures should eliminate any misunderstanding about this. Here are just a few examples:

- *"For if that which is **done away** was glorious, much more that which remaineth is glorious."* (2 Corinthians 3:11)
- *"And not as Moses, which put a veil over his face, that the children of Israel could not stedfastly look to the end of **that which is abolished**."* (2 Corinthians 3:13)

- "**Blotting out** the handwriting of ordinances that was against us, which was contrary to us, and took it out of the way, nailing it to his cross." (Colossians 2:14)

  (**NOTE**: Strong's definition: to smear out; to obliterate.)

- "Having **abolished** in his flesh the enmity, even the law of commandments contained in ordinances; for to make in himself of twain one new man, so making peace." (Ephesians 2:15)

- "In that he saith, A new covenant, **he hath made the first old**. Now that which **decayeth** and **waxeth old** is ready to **vanish away**." (Hebrews 8:13)

- "But after that faith is come, we are **no longer under a schoolmaster**." (Galatians 3:25)

- "For Christ is the **end of the law** for righteousness to every one that believeth." Romans 10:4)

- "**Cast out the bondwoman and her son**." (Galatians 4:30)

- "**All things are lawful for m**e, but all things are not expedient: **all things are lawful for me**, but all things edify not. Let no man seek his own, but every man another's wealth." (1 Corinthians 10:23-24)

- "But now we are **delivered from the law**, that being dead wherein we were held;

that we should serve in newness of spirit, and not in the oldness of the letter." (Romans 7:6)

- *"For there is verily a **disannulling of the commandment going before** for the **weakness** and **unprofitableness** thereof."* (Hebrews 7:18)

  (**NOTE**: Strong's definition of "annul:" to annihilate; make void – as legal rights, laws, established rules. Strong's definition of "disannul:" to annul completely; cancel; put away.)

- *"Then said he, Lo, I come to do thy will, O God. He **taketh away** the first that he may establish the second."* (Hebrews 10:9)

If a mortgage agreement is fulfilled or satisfied, it is done, complete, no longer in effect, and put away. All the terms and conditions have been met. As long as one "jot or tittle" of the mortgage remains unsatisfied, the debtor is still under obligation to all of its provisions. But once the debtor can say, "It is finished," it no longer has any legal hold over him.

HALLELUJAH!

The obligation is already fulfilled, and you hold full legal title to the home. There's nothing you can do to make it any more paid off than it already is. Should someone come to you and instruct or demand that you continue making payments once the mortgage is satisfied, the only reason you might do so is because of **ignorance** or **intimidation**. This can only happen if you are not sufficiently acquainted with the provisions of the mortgage agreement and fully confident of the fact that, once the terms are fulfilled, the home cannot be legally taken from you.

Continuing to make payments once the mortgage terms have been satisfied or fulfilled is, in fact, a **self-imposed bondage**. It doesn't give you any more title or privilege than you already have. All it does is drain you of resources you need not be expending and frustrate you because you know that you shouldn't really be making those payments anyhow.

Another reason why one might continue to make payments on the fulfilled mortgage is if he is not fully convinced that the legal system will uphold his claim. In the spiritual realm, if we are not sufficiently acquainted with Jesus, our Advocate, we could have doubts about whether our stand against the claims of the law is valid. **If we are not fully aware of what He accomplished on the cross and that His name is above every other name, we might very well succumb to the incursions of one presenting false claims against our lives. This is exactly what the enemy seeks to do against every blood-bought child of God. If he can keep us in bondage to the law, we will be diverted from attending to the plan and call of God on our lives.**

FRUSTRATING THE GRACE OF GOD

"I do not frustrate the grace of God: for if righteousness come by the law, then Christ is dead in vain." (Galatians 2:21)

When one conveys a gift, there is an expectation that the gift will be received with appreciation. For the recipient to scowl or scoff at a gift would be most unexpected and unwelcome. We could say that such a response would "frustrate the grace" (unmerited favor) of the giver. In Galatians 2:21, Paul says that this is exactly what happens when a Christian, after receiving Jesus and enjoying the good things of God's grace, decides to return to the tenets and trappings of the law.

Taking the above paid-off mortgage scenario one step further – let's assume that someone paid the mortgage off for you as a gift. For you to continue making payments beyond this point would not only be foolish – it would also be an insult to the one from whom the gift was given. It says that you don't really believe the mortgage is paid and is, in fact, **unbelief**. It is unthankfulness and a true insult.

This is precisely what happens when we elect to forsake faith and return to the law. In effect, we say to God, "Thanks for sending Your son to die for me but I can handle it from here." The Bible refers to this as having "fallen from grace." In his letter to the Galatians, Paul put it this way:

"Christ is become of no effect unto you, whosoever of you are justified by the law; ye are fallen from grace."
(Galatians 5:4)

In other words, if a gift has been given to you but you reject it, choosing, instead, to go out and work so you can buy the item yourself, you have fallen from grace, i.e., you have chosen works instead of grace.

What a terrible thought. Yet, this is the reality of such action. In Hebrews 10:29, such denial of our Savior is described more specifically:

"Of how much sorer punishment, suppose ye, shall he be thought worthy, who hath trodden under foot the Son of God, and hath counted the blood of the covenant, wherewith he was sanctified, an unholy thing, and hath done despite unto the Spirit of grace?"

Notice these three things:

- **Treading Jesus under foot**
- **Counting the blood of the covenant unholy**
- **Insulting the Spirit of grace**

These are serious charges and certainly not ones with which any Jesus-loving person would want to be associated. We are free to choose to have our eternal destiny determined by our own merits. But to make such a choice is to turn from, reject, and frustrate the grace freely given to us by God.

Current day torah teaching says that a Christian doesn't obey the law because he is required to but because he wants to. It is a way, we are told, of walking out our righteousness and of showing our love for God. Using the above mortgage example, however, we can see that, once again, we can't add anything to a fulfilled commitment. Attempting to do so is an insult to our heavenly Father – not an act of love.

THE LAW VERSUS FAITH:
It's One or the Other

Paul's teaching makes it very clear that **the law and faith are mutually exclusive**. In other words, you either have one or the other. This is most disconcerting for those who would have us believe that we are to somehow obey the law by faith. To close the door on such thinking, Paul says:

"And if by grace, then is it no more of works: otherwise grace is no more grace. But if it be of works, then is it no more grace: otherwise work is no more work." (Romans 11:6)

The choice is ours. We can either live by the law or by faith. But an attempt to do both is an affront to God's gift of grace to us. **There's no fence straddling here**. God's grace doesn't need our help. Paul made this clear when he said:

"And the law is not of faith: but, the man that doeth them shall live in them." (Galatians 3:12)

The decision to walk either by the law or by faith is ours to make. What is not an option is for us to walk in both places simultaneously. If we choose the law, which is fulfilled by works then, as Paul said, we "shall live in them." That is, we are then required to fulfill the law completely or suffer the associated penalties. If we fail in one point of the law, we become guilty of breaking the whole law.

Without an accurate understanding of **how** Jesus' death purged our sins (i.e., by putting away the law – 2 Corinthians 3:14), we become easy prey for religious sounding teachings and doctrines that undermine the power of His precious, shed blood. It is essential, therefore, to understand both the purpose and the attributes of the law if we are to steer clear of this subtle and seductive snare. Once we properly understand the law, we recognize that as long as it remains in place, sin is still imputed.

"For until the law sin was in the world: but sin is not imputed when there is no law." (Romans 5:13)

Only by the removal of the law are we free from sin and its penalty. Here we see the true miracle and power of the cross. A proper understanding is essential if we are to be fully set free from the captivity of sin.

If Jesus took the law *"out of the way"* (Colossians 2:14), so that it could no longer hold us captive to sin, far be it from us to invite it back into our lives. Yet, this is the deceptive snare into which many sincere believers are walking. By re-establishing the law's authority in their lives, they are restoring the very thing that Jesus came to deliver them from. (Romans 7:6) In Galatians 2:18, the Apostle Paul said:

> *"For if I build again the things which I destroyed, **I make myself a transgressor**."*

With the law fulfilled and no longer holding us captive to sin, the only sin remaining to beset us is our own decision to raise it back up and give it authority in and over our lives. This becomes a most perilous choice since, as we saw in Hebrews 10:29, by doing so, we tread underfoot the Son of God, we count the blood of the covenant wherewith we were sanctified an unholy thing, and we insult the Spirit of grace.

The book of Galatians is devoted almost exclusively to admonishing the believers to be on guard and to avoid those who come giving instruction that they should obey the commands of the law. Paul said they were:

> *"Unawares brought in, who came in privily to spy out our liberty which we have in Christ Jesus, that they might **bring us into bondage**."* (Galatians 2:4)

The reason there is so much difficulty comprehending this truth is because of the abundance of renegade, religious spirits running rampant within the church that have deceived Christians into believing that they must walk in both places. This is exactly the type of deception which Paul warned us to be vigilant towards. If we allow these untruths to come in and steal our liberty for which Jesus died, then we will return to the bondage of the law and be stuck in a performance/works way of living.

OUR RESPONSE (RELATIONSHIP) TO THE OLD COVENANT

A religious mindset will always keep us from apprehending the true power of God. The word "religion" comes from the Greek word *"religio"* which, by definition, means "a return to bondage." This is why "religion" is, perhaps, one of the greatest weapons of Satan's arsenal against the committed believer. The person with a true heart for God desires the joy of His presence above all else. For Satan to try to divert such a person with temptations of blatant sin would be a waste of his time. But to tempt that person with religious diversions is much more likely to succeed. This is why it becomes essential that we not assimilate teaching just because it sounds spiritual. First and foremost, we must always let the Word speak for itself and listen with unbiased, attentive ears. If we will do this, the matter of understanding what place the old covenant has in our lives becomes quite simple.

Within the Galatian church were those who taught that Christians must obey the law. Paul was clearly not of this persuasion. Aware of how contentious the issue was among the Jewish believers, Paul first emphasizes that what he is teaching is not a product of man's wisdom but, rather, a revelation received directly from God:

> *"But I certify you, brethren, that the gospel which was preached of me is not after man. For I neither received it of man, neither was I taught it, but by the revelation of Jesus Christ."* (Galatians 1:11-12)

In Galatians, chapter 4, Paul speaks to the issue regarding the relationship between the law and the believer. Beginning in verse 21, he addresses these false teachers in no uncertain terms by saying:

> *"Tell me, ye that desire to be under the law, do ye not hear the law?"*

In a paraphrase: here you are professing to be teachers of the law and you don't even understand what the law is saying. He then goes on to explain the relationship of the believer to the law:

> *"For it is written, that Abraham had two sons, the one by a bondmaid, the other by a freewoman. But he who was of the bondwoman was born after the flesh; but he of the freewoman was by promise. Which things are an allegory: for these are the two covenants; the one from the mount Sinai, which gendereth to bondage, which is Agar. For this Agar is mount Sinai in Arabia, and answereth to Jerusalem which now is, and is in bondage with her children. But Jerusalem which is above is free, which is the mother of us all. For it is written, Rejoice, thou barren that bearest not; break forth and cry, thou that travailest not: for the desolate hath many more*

children than she which hath an husband. Now we, brethren, as Isaac was, are the children of promise. But as then he that was born after the flesh persecuted him that was born after the Spirit, even so it is now. Nevertheless what saith the scripture? Cast out the bondwoman and her son: for the son of the bondwoman shall not be heir with the son of the freewoman. So then, brethren, we are not children of the bondwoman, but of the free."
(Galatians 4:22-31)

CAN IT GET ANY CLEARER THAN THIS?

In case a question remains, let's look at the Greek word *"ekballo"* which is translated in the King James: "cast out." Strong's Concordance defines the term this way: "**drive out, expel, thrust out, put out, send away.**" Using the allegory that Paul presents, it is clear that "cast out" is what we are to do with the law (the bondwoman) and everything it has produced or wants to produce in our lives (her son) outside of driving us to our knees before the cross of Christ.

Paul uses an allegory here describing the law as the bondmaid and the promise as the freewoman. Notice that the covenant from Mount Sinai (the law) "gendereth" to bondage. This word means "begets," "leads to," or "brings forth." As long as we are of the law, we are in bondage **because bondage is what the law produces. To say that we must fulfill the law by the power of the Spirit is a contradiction and totally inconsistent with the teachings of the New Testament**.

The New Testament puts the believer in a higher place than the law just as complying with the law of aerodynamics can bring us to a higher place than obeying the law of gravity. One can obey or be perfectly in subjection to the law of gravity and still never be able to fly. Flight requires adherence to a totally different set of laws. So, also, it is in the Spirit. The law is truth just as the law of gravity is truth. **But not until we recognize and align ourselves with the higher truths can we soar above the carnal and into heavenly places**.

You have probably heard that any time we see the word "therefore" in Scripture, we need to know what it is there for. This is certainly a wise question to ask concerning Galatians 5:1 which says:

> "Stand fast **therefore** in the liberty where-with Christ hath made us free, and be not entangled again with the yoke of bondage."

The "therefore" is there to tell us that, because the law is behind us and no longer has the power to bring us under its bondage, we are now free to walk *"in the liberty wherewith Christ hath made us free."* The law is, in fact, a *"yoke of bondage"* that will work in opposition to the grace of God if we purpose to hold on to it and try to fulfill it in our lives. Because we now have become the righteousness of God, the law no longer pertains to us.

> *"Knowing this, that the law is not made for a righteous man, but for the lawless and disobedient, for the ungodly and for sinners."* (1 Timothy 1:9)

To remove any doubt about his strong stand on this issue and to be sure that the disciples were not being hypocritical between what they were teaching and what they were practicing, Paul took Peter to task for the double standard he was presenting:

> *"But when Peter was come to Antioch, I withstood him to the face, because he was to be blamed. For before that certain came from James, he did eat with the Gentiles: but when they were come, he withdrew and separated himself, fearing them which were of the circumcision. And the other Jews dissembled (acted hypocritically in concert with one another) likewise with him; insomuch that Barnabas also was carried away with their dissimulation (hypocrisy). But when I saw that they walked not uprightly according to the truth of the gospel, I said unto Peter before them all, If thou, being a Jew, livest after the manner of Gentiles, and not as do the Jews, why compellest thou the Gentiles to live as do the Jews?"*
> (Galatians 2:11-14)

Paul was continually taken to task by many believing Jews who still wanted to hold on to the law, who did not recognize the law's design and purpose as described above. In Acts, chapter 15, we see that the dispute over this matter stirred up such a fury in Antioch that Paul and Barnabas had to return to Jerusalem to get it resolved before continuing on in their ministry. Seemingly, when they began sharing about all that took place in Asia, some of the Pharisees also challenged what they were teaching.

> *"But there rose up certain of the sect of the Pharisees which believed, saying, That it was needful to circumcise them, and to command them to keep the law of Moses."* (Acts 15:5)

Peter first responded saying:

> *"Now therefore why tempt ye God, to put a yoke upon the neck of the disciples, which neither our fathers nor we were able to bear?"* (Acts 15:10)

Paul and Barnabas then shared more about their ministry after which James said:

> *"Wherefore my sentence is, that we trouble not them, which from among the Gentiles are turned to God: But that we write unto them, that they abstain from pollutions of idols, and from fornication, and from things strangled, and from blood."* (Acts 15:19-20)

The apostles and elders agreed. With the matter resolved, they prepared a letter regarding their decision and sent it out with Paul and Barnabas along with Judas Barsabbas and Silas back to Antioch to announce their determination. Here is what their letter said:

> *"The apostles and elders and brethren send greeting unto the brethren which are of the Gentiles in Antioch and Syria and Cilicia. Forasmuch as we have heard, that certain which went out from us have troubled you with words, subverting your souls, saying, Ye must be circumcised, and*

keep the law: **to whom we gave no such commandment***: It seemed good unto us, being assembled with one accord, to send chosen men unto you with our beloved Barnabas and Paul, Men that have hazarded their lives for the name of our Lord Jesus Christ. We have sent therefore Judas and Silas, who shall also tell you the same things by mouth. For it seemed good to the Holy Ghost, and to us, to lay upon you no greater burden than these necessary things; That ye abstain from meats offered to idols, and from blood, and from things strangled, and from fornication: from which if ye keep yourselves, ye shall do well. Fare ye well."* (Acts 15:23-29)

HIGHER GROUND

By now, the question most likely before you is: "Well, if the law and its demands are behind us, what is it that keeps us in line?" In a word, the answer is "**love**." The commandment Jesus gave was to **love one another**.

> *"A new commandment I give unto you, That ye love one another; as I have loved you, that ye also love one another."*
> (John 13:34)

But he did far more than give us the commandment to love. He also gave us the **desire** and **ability** to love each other. When we walk in love, we are in a place high above the *"weak and beggarly elements"* (Galatians 4:9) of the law.

The law is directed toward and limited by the flesh. (Hebrews 9:13; Romans 8:3) The law makes demands the flesh cannot fulfill and holds us captive to it. The displacement of the old covenant by the new lifts helpless man out of the terrible bondage and hopelessness faced through the law and gives us a new heart of love whereby our lives rise up into a high place totally unconceivable to and unattainable by the flesh.

> *"But the fruit of the Spirit is love, joy, peace, longsuffering, gentleness, good-*

> ness, faith, meekness, temperance: against such there is no law." (Galatians 5:22-23)

Never underestimate the deceitfulness and wickedness of the flesh. The reason we are so prone and willing to forsake the goodness, mercy, and grace God brings to us through Jesus is because the natural man is always looking for a way to regain a foothold in the life of the believer. We like the law and its demands because it offers a way by which we can compare ourselves to others – particularly those whose lives don't seem to match up to ours – and raise ourselves above them.

> *"The heart is deceitful above all things, and desperately wicked: who can know it?"* (Jeremiah 17:9)

Perhaps a good way to see the difference between the Law of Moses and the Law of Love is through a parable:

A man hires a young woman to work for him as a housekeeper. He prepares a list of duties for her to perform and checks to be sure they are all being done properly. The man is very strict about what he wants done and deducts from her pay for failures to comply. The checklist review creates a fear in her and becomes a bondage to her. Down the line, the man comes to love the housekeeper and takes her as his wife. When this happens, a change takes place. The man no longer looks to her with a checklist in his hand and the woman joyfully performs household chores above and beyond what the man ever expected because of her love for him. Neither does his wife go back and prepare a checklist for him to review each day when he returns from work. To do so would be an affront to the man who chose to take her as his wife.

If we fail to identify and comprehend this vital distinction between the law and grace we miss, completely, the entire mission and purpose for which Jesus came to earth. It would appear that this lack of understanding (or our plain rebellion against the whole concept of love) is the reason why, within the body of Christ, the divorce rate is no different than that of the world. Believers have simply failed to comprehend what love really is. Instead of allowing the spirit of love that God implanted within our being when we became born again to rule and govern our lives, husbands and wives continue to look at one another with "measuring sticks." One is forever evaluating and criticizing the performance of the other.

We live "under the law," one to the other, and we reap the fruit thereof. The pride, anger, resentment, and bitterness that arises from the dissatisfaction with the performance of our spouse results in the "death" of the marriage. All this comes about because the love, mercy, and grace that Jesus gave to us when He ushered in the new covenant is nowhere to be found in the marriage. Should we be surprised, then, that Christian divorce rates match those of unbelievers? Hardly!

SUMMING IT ALL UP

As we can see from the above discussion, the contention that arises from the opposing messages of law and grace is not unique to our time. Its origins go all the way back to the time of Jesus when, through His finished work on the cross, the reality of God's grace was a glaring affront to the works of the law that emanate from performance and pride. It is, in fact, the true essence of spiritual warfare. This is why Peter refers to Jesus as a *"stone of stumbling, and a rock of offence."* (1 Peter 2:8) The concept of grace is offensive to the natural man and the thought of having no way to glory in fleshly performance and accomplishments is repulsive to the flesh.

> *"But God hath chosen the foolish things of the world to confound the wise; and God hath chosen the weak things of the world to confound the things which are mighty; And base things of the world, and things which are despised, hath God chosen, yea, and things which are not, to bring to nought things that are: That no flesh should glory in his presence."*
> (1 Corinthians 1:27-29)

Is it any wonder, then, that the enemy of our souls would relentlessly attempt to convince us that measured performance is key to walking uprightly before God? No one was confronted with this issue more than the Apostle Paul. A brief review of his background reveals why he was the one chosen of God to receive such a great revelation regarding God's dispensation of grace.

Of all those called of God to carry the Gospel message, Paul, more than any, had reason to boast as an adherent to the torah. He was steeped in the law both through heritage and in lifestyle and derived a great sense of purpose from striving to fulfill it flawlessly:

> *"Circumcised the eighth day, of the stock of Israel, of the tribe of Benjamin, an Hebrew of the Hebrews; as touching the law, a Pharisee; concerning zeal, persecuting the church; touching the righteousness which is in the law, blameless."* (Philippians 3:5-6)

When it came to the law, Paul had every "I" dotted and every "T" crossed. Yet, despite the high level of perfection to which he met the law's demands, his ultimate realization was that it was all for naught.

> *"Yea doubtless, and I count all things but loss for the excellency of the knowledge of Christ Jesus my Lord: for whom I have suffered the loss of all things, and do count them but dung, that I may win Christ."* (Philippians 3:8)

All the striving regarding the law was in the past. It was no more a part of his life. Paul recognized it to be futile and worthless and nothing more than history. God had now made possible a new and better way, and he chose to walk in it and leave the old ways of the law behind. He had been liberated from the law and its demands to walk in a new and glorious way that was far and above anything the law could even begin to offer. There was a better prize ahead in the "high calling" that God had given him.

"Brethren, I count not myself to have apprehended: but this one thing I do, forgetting those things which are behind, and reaching forth unto those things which are before, I press toward the mark for the prize of the high calling of God in Christ Jesus." (Philippians 3:13-14)

Clearly the matter of the law and grace was not an issue for Paul. It was over, settled, and done with. A new and better way had come.

"For what the law could not do, in that it was weak through the flesh, God sending his own Son in the likeness of sinful flesh, and for sin, condemned sin in the flesh: that the righteousness of the law might be fulfilled in us, who walk not after the flesh, but after the Spirit." (Romans 8:3-4)

The law had done its work by showing Paul the vanity and futility of all fleshly strivings:

"Wherefore the law was our schoolmaster to bring us unto Christ, that we might be justified by faith. But after that faith is come, we are no longer under a schoolmaster." (Galatians 3:24-25)

Now he was free to embrace the glorious salvation bestowed upon him by the mercy and grace of his heavenly Father who sent His only begotten Son to shed His blood and die for his sins. To continue to strive to comply with the law would be to reject God's most precious gift and to discredit Jesus' sacrifice for him. This, Paul knew, would be a serious reproach to the Gospel message.

This brings us back to our opening comments. The process of redemption to which the Old Testament pertained was only part of the salvation plan. We have seen in the foregoing pages that the summary purpose of the law was to make us aware of our need for a Savior. The law was not only a wall between man's relationship with God; it was also a wall between the Jew and the Gentile. Through His death on the cross, Jesus removed this wall between man's relationship with God:

> *"And Jesus cried with a loud voice, and gave up the ghost. And the veil of the temple was rent in twain from the top to the bottom."* (Mark 15:37-38)

... as well as making a way for an end to the division that stood between Jew and Gentile.

> *"For he is our peace, who hath made both one, and hath broken down the middle wall of partition between us; Having abolished in his flesh the enmity, even the law of commandments contained in ordinances; for to make in himself of twain one new man, so making peace; And that*

he might reconcile both unto God in one body by the cross, so making peace." (Ephesians 2:14-15)

So, while all the teachings about the need for the believer to obey the law have a nice, spiritual ring to them, it should be very evident to any who would hear the full counsel of God that the law is what Jesus came to deliver us from.

"But now we are delivered from the law, that being dead wherein we were held; that we should serve in newness of spirit, and not in the oldness of the letter." (Romans 7:6)

By lifting up or restoring in our lives that which Jesus fulfilled, i.e., the law, we, by our own choice, make ourselves transgressors (Galatians 2:18) and leave between the Jew and Gentile the very wall that Jesus came to tear down. This is most paradoxical since so many Christian believers today are attempting to bring about a unity between the two through the use of the law. Clearly this is in total opposition to what the Bible teaches.

Jesus' fulfillment of the law and the New Testament emphasis on grace through faith does not diminish the importance of the law in making a sinner aware of his lost condition. The law still serves to convict the unbeliever of his need for a Savior. This is why it is vital that the Ten Commandments remain at the core of our national legal framework. Without them, society will continue to degenerate as people rationalize their wicked behavior more and more.

If there is no law, there is no means by which the lost can see their need for salvation. Jesus' work on the cross was to remove the burden of the law from the believer. But once it has accomplished this, the work of the law is finished in that person's life.

LOVING MEMORIES

This is one of the many poems that Warren wrote. He loved writing sweet poems for me, his Sweet Love.

"HAPPY 45TH MY SWEET LOVE"

*While many marriages
May not survive,
Ours is still strong
At—WOW—forty-five.*

*Rockin and Rollin
Over the years
Sometimes with smiles;
Sometimes with tears.*

*Whatever might happen,
We give it our best,
Then, trusting in Jesus,
We soon find our rest.*

*He's clearly the truth,
The life and the way,
He blesses our lives
With each passing day.*

*As our love grows—
more and more
Our aging bodies
Seem to hit the floor.*

*But Jesus Christ
Is always regal
He renews our youth
Like the eagle.*

A SONG WARREN WROTE
(before he got sick)

"THROUGH YOUR WORD"

VERSE 1

When my faith is weak, still your face I seek, knowing that your love will not fail me.

In my darkest hour, by your word of power, I will trust and not be afraid.

CHORUS

Through your word and your grace, I will seek your face, till your work in me is done.

By your love and through faith, I will run the race, till the good fight of faith is won.

VERSE 2

You are Christ the king, life and rest you bring, when the storms of life come against me.

Grace and peace is mine, through the one true vine. Lord, I praise your glorious name.

CHORUS AGAIN

VERSE 3

As a mustard grain, growing through my pain
Speaking words of life that will heal,
Speaking to the mountain I feel.

CHORUS AGAIN

VERSE 4

Trusting evermore, Knocking at each door
Watching for the Lord to reveal.

CHORUS AGAIN

Warren enjoyed playing the piano. It was one of his many ways of relaxing.

EULOGY: MY DAD
by Warren's son, David Schoder

I'd like to thank you all for coming here today to honor my father and to support my mother.

You are all here because you knew my dad in different ways. And today as we get to share with each other the Warren that "we" knew ... we will be sharing similar stories of his true nature.

Many of you know him as a man of faith, a believer of God's promises.

My father was a man who made honesty, kindness, and integrity his daily practice.

He was a man who was dedicated and committed to his family, married and faithful to my mother for fifty-five years.

He was our rock.

He was our provider.

He was our source of strength.

He brought a sense of balance, true wisdom, and undying stability to my family.

He was a practical adviser and a patient listener, always supportive, gentle, and kind.

As a child, I have fond memories of summers here on the lake, a tradition in our family that was important for him to share and continue with us.

It has been an enduring legacy coming up on almost 100 years, that allowed us to spend countless summers here with our grandparents, aunts, uncles, cousins, and extended family.

These summer trips were so special to us that we were always so excited to get here, and so sad to leave. I still feel that way to this day. And I believe that I share that sentiment with my whole family.

As all of our family grows, that sentiment continues to grow and the bonds between us get stronger. I'm eternally grateful that my dad made those trips possible, and that it was important to him to share with us.

As a teen, my father helped my sister and I with purchasing our first vehicles. When I got my driving permit, he was diligent about instructing me in the ways of basic vehicle maintenance. Checking tires for air and levels for fluids, but most importantly, how to change my own oil. With a checklist on how to do so, making sure I was aware of the steps necessary to do this successfully.

Looking back, I've realized how this early lesson really prepared me for so much more than just changing my oil, but gave me an insight toward my future independence, helping me to understand that there are wrong ways to do things and a process to getting them done right.

My sister and I just had a smile and a laugh about the checklist he made for us to use whenever purchasing a vehicle. Extremely detailed and thorough. Extremely practical advice.

He was conservative and thrifty in his acquisitions. He loved a good deal. In his retirement years, he loved to "bulk" shop. As we all used to joke that my mom was the one who loved to "buy more to save more." I feel he inherited those traits from fifty-five years of marriage with her.

He was an organized hoarder. He had labeled containers, boxes, and locations for these possessions. Well sorted, curated, for those times where "who knows I may need these someday." And he knew just where to find them when he did.

He was a stakeholder at Harbor Freight, and became a bigtime investor at Amazon.

He was a practical problem solver. I feel the traits I inherited from observing him have helped me with many of the projects, problems, and obstacles I've had to face, usually leading me to a healthy resolve or in some cases, compromise or redirect.

A bit of advice he gave me more than once, when I've felt stuck or undecided, was that even when you don't know what to do or which direction to go in, it's best just to move forward ... to do something.

Sometimes there are no right or definitive answers in the moment that we are seeking them.

My father was not unblemished or perfect by any means. As a man of God ... a faith walker and believer, he still had his weaknesses. In the more recent months, I began to notice his sense of worry, obligation to others, and a disappointment of letting us down. There were things that were just beyond his control.

We were able to share some positive and reinforcing texts together before I realized his true infirmities. I was adamant to help reinforce his faith by omitting "worry" from his mental practice, for him to be able to rest in the unknown and the unseen.

And having been on the receiving end of scripture he would share with me at appropriate times in my life, I for once was able to share one that had always deeply resonated with me.

And now I'd like to share those verses with you (Matthew 6:25-34 / NAS):

> *"Therefore I tell you, do not worry about your life, what you will eat [or drink], or about your body, what you will wear. Is not life more than food and the body more than clothing?*
>
> *Look at the birds in the sky; they do not sow or reap, they gather nothing into barns, yet your heavenly Father feeds them. Are not you more important than they?*
>
> *Can any of you by worrying add a single moment to your life-span?*
>
> *Why are you anxious about clothes? Learn from the way the wild flowers grow. They do not work or spin.*
>
> *But I tell you that not even Solomon in all his splendor was clothed like one of them.*
>
> *If God so clothes the grass of the field, which grows today and is thrown into the*

oven tomorrow, will he not much more provide for you, O you of little faith?

So do not worry and say, 'What are we to eat?' or 'What are we to drink?' or 'What are we to wear?'

All these things the pagans seek. Your heavenly Father knows that you need them all.

But seek first the kingdom [of God] and his righteousness,[c] and all these things will be given you besides.

Do not worry about tomorrow; tomorrow will take care of itself. Sufficient for a day is its own evil."

I will miss him not just because he was a loving father, and for the truths I've just spoken of him, but also because I can honestly say there are not many men left in the world like him. I'm sure many of you will agree.

A good friend reached out to send his condolences the other day and said, "Warren was a class act, and they just don't make them like that anymore."

Thank you again for being here to celebrate the life of a truly amazing human, my father, Warren Rex Schoder.

I love you, Dad.

Warren and son David

A LOVING NOTE
from Warren's grandson,
Noah Schoder

As humans thrust into this life of infinite complexity, hardship and love ...

We are brought into this world with a great fear of death.

For ourselves, yes, but far greater for those around us who we have spent our lives with.

Those who live on bear the loss of others, but we also live on with the examples they have set and memories of them we will forever cherish.

As we share our love throughout our lives, it ripples outward to others.

And even in passing those ripples continue to change others' lives and the world for the better.

Warren, my grandfather, created as many ripples as a storm on a lake, or the tide on the shore.

Not only will his love ripple for eternity, but so shall his faith.

As he lived with faith, he has passed beyond with a faith in the Lord so strong many here would agree it was contagious.

Till now, I've never been so sure that someone would be welcomed into the gates of heaven so swiftly.

Warren and grandson Noah

BIOGRAPHICAL SUMMARY

WARREN SCHODER
(June 21, 1942—November 5, 2023)

Warren Schoder was born in Jersey City, New Jersey. From the beginning, he spent his summers at the family cabin in Hague, New York, near Lake George, but in 2017, moved there permanently. It was a favorite spot for his main hobby: boating. He often said he never really dreamed of living in Hague, until he moved there—then he realized, "It was the dream he never thought he had." He was a Bible teacher and founder of Royal Bounty Financial, a Christian company dedicated to helping the body of Christ "come out" of this world's economic and monetary system and to handle their finances in a sound, biblical manner.

Warren held a B.S. degree in Business Management from Fairleigh Dickinson University. He also graduated from the Graduate School of Savings Banking at Brown University and the Executive Development School at the University of Massachusetts. He was Vice President of bank operations for a large New Jersey thrift institution for sixteen years, serving as the executive of the bank's data processing and general operations functions.

After leaving banking to fulfill a ministry call, Warren completed the Gospel Crusade Institute of Ministry (IOM) training school at Christian

Retreat in Bradenton, Florida, in December of 1983. Following this, he joined Gospel Crusade as General Manager during which time he taught both in the IOM and in the adult church education program at Christian Retreat Family Church. In 1987, he was ordained by the Gospel Crusade Ministerial Fellowship. He served as an elder at Christian Retreat from 1985 to 1995, and as a Gospel Crusade board advisor from 1986-1994.

Warren and Margo started a billboard ministry called "Declare His Glory" on major highways in Florida, Colorado, and Wyoming. Many thousands of people were presented with essential biblical truths as they drove by the signs.

In 1993, Warren left Gospel Crusade and becoming certified as an estate planning advisor, established his own living trust business.

In 1995, God led him into a deeper revelation of end-times economic events and began revealing how those who heeded God's instructions to be set apart in their financial affairs would be spared the economic devastation that has already taken place in many parts of the world and is presently manifesting in the United States. According to Warren's teaching, this is an indication that the third seal of Revelation is being opened.

In 1995, Warren began teaching believers about the dishonest weights and measures employed in the world's financial system and the snares within it that will entrap all those who fail to "come out" of it.

In 1997, he started his business, Royal Bounty Financial, to teach the body of Christ about honest money systems and to enable them to become established by using sound, biblical money planning techniques.

In 2004, he and his wife Margo moved to New Mexico where they started a home church, also called "Declare His Glory."

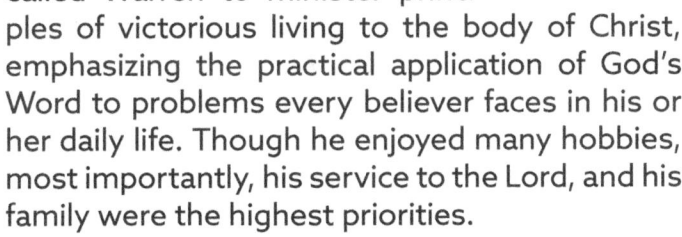

In the broader sense, God called Warren to minister principles of victorious living to the body of Christ, emphasizing the practical application of God's Word to problems every believer faces in his or her daily life. Though he enjoyed many hobbies, most importantly, his service to the Lord, and his family were the highest priorities.

Warren and Margo were married in 1968. Warren passed on to his heavenly reward on November 5, 2023. Margo is currently living in upstate New York. They were blessed with three children: Susan, David, and Amber, a special addition to their family. They are grandparents to five boys: Matthew, Noah, Evan, Luke, and Gavin.

"Sweet Memories"

PHOTO ALBUM

Warren's parents Erlo and Helen,
Warren and his brother, Barry

Warren (right), brother Barry,
and sister Carol

This a picture of Warren in 1968, after his first bank promotion.

Warren and his dad Erlo. Warren served in the United States Air Force Reserves.

Warren (right), brother Barry, and sister Carol

Warren (right) and his brother Barry

Warren and his sister Carol

On our wedding day, December 22, 1968

Warren and Margo at a banking function, 1969

Warren and Margo dressed for the
High Ballers night at the cabin at Lake George.

Bob Timberlake – Market Street Mission.
He was the director of missions in New Jersey.

Warren and Margo ministering in the Tuguegarao, Cagayan, Philippines in 1989 (they were invited by Claudio and Hosanna Cortez)

Warren loved to share God's Word with people.

Warren's horses that he loved—
Katrina, Buddy, and White Foot

Warren loved boating on Lake George.

Warren had his pilot's license and this was his first solo flight.

Warren had a good friend who was retiring from United Airlines. He asked him to join him on his last flight on the 747 into the Denver airport.

Warren loved vacation at Lake George with his family. This is one of our many porch pictures.

Warren's favorite past time was being out on the boat at Lake George.

Family meant the world to Warren.

Warren and son David

Warren and daughter Susan

PHOTO ALBUM

Warren with his son David and daughter Susan at a friend's wedding

Warren and daughter Susan in Colorado

Amber, adopted-in-love daughter

Our daughter Susan's family
(Grandson Matthew, Scott our son-in-love,
Susan, & grandsons Luke and Evan).

This is a picture of Warren, Margo and grandsons Matthew, Noah and Evan at the beach.

Our grandchildren:
Matthew, Noah and Evan

Grandson Gavin

This is a side by side picture of Warren and his grandson Evan when they were around the same age wearing their cowboy gear.

Grandson Matthew

Grandson Noah

Grandson Evan Clay

Grandson Matthew and Warren using the backhoe for a project.

Warren's boat

Warren enjoyed being able to wear his cowboy hat while attending a cowboy wedding.

Warren in the Caribbean on one of the many cruises we enjoyed

Warren loved cruising. This is from one of our many trips.

Warren and Margo enjoying a hot spring in Colorado

Celebrating Memorial Day at Lake George

Warren enjoying Lake George

Warren was a huge fan of the TV show "Walker Texas Ranger."

Our special friends and family—
the Stevenson's from Florida

Our extended family from New Mexico:
Chris, Celina and miracle baby, Janae.

Warren renewing Chris and Celina's marriage.

Warren dedicating a young couple's baby.

Pastor Skip and Janet Trembley, our pastors

Special friends, Pastors Phil & Jannette Derstine, Christian Retreat

Christian Retreat, Bradenton, Florida

Warren with his "SWEET LOVE" Margo

www.ingramcontent.com/pod-product-compliance
Lightning Source LLC
Chambersburg PA
CBHW060839050426
42453CB00008B/754